BUILDING ROBOTS
ROBOTIC ENGINEERS

DANIEL R. FAUST

New York

Published in 2016 by The Rosen Publishing Group, Inc.
29 East 21st Street, New York, NY 10010

First Edition

Editor: Caitlin McAneney
Book Design: Katelyn Heinle

Photo Credits: Cover, p. 7 Hero Images/Getty Images; p. 5 (Bumblebee) Shamleen/Shutterstock.com; p. 5 (RoboCop) Joe Seer/Shutterstock.com; p. 5 (C-3PO) Clemens Bilan/Getty Images Entertainment/ Getty Images; p. 5 (T-800) YOSHIKAZU TSUNO/AFP/Getty Images; p. 6 Imagno/Hulton Archive/Getty Images; p. 9 (inset) Erik Möller/Wikimedia Commons; p. 9 (main) Georgios Kollidas/Shutterstock.com; p. 10 Hulton Archive/Archive Photos/Getty Images; p. 12 science photo/Shutterstock.com; p. 13 Vinne/ Shutterstock.com; p. 14 Getty Images/Handout/Hulton Archive/Getty Images; p. 15 Ociacia/Shutterstock. com; p. 17 (top) wellphoto/Shutterstock.com; p. 17 (bottom) Pieter Beens/Shutterstock.com; p. 19 vladimir salman/Shutterstock.com; p. 21 Douglas McFadd/Getty Images News/Getty Images; p. 23 ilterriorm/ Shutterstock.com; p. 24 Christopher Hallaran/Shutterstock.com; p. 25 John Lund/Blend Images/Getty Images; p. 27 (top) Colin Anderson/Photographer's Choice/Getty Images; p. 27 (bottom) Scott Nelson/ Getty Images News/Getty Images; p. 29 Goran Bogicevic/Shutterstock.com; p. 30 Thomas Barwick/ Iconica/Getty Images.

Library of Congress Cataloging-in-Publication Data

Faust, Daniel R., author.
 Building robots : robotic engineers / Daniel R. Faust.
    pages cm. — (Engineers rule!)
 ISBN 978-1-5081-4540-0 (pbk.)
 ISBN 978-1-5081-4541-7 (6 pack)
 ISBN 978-1-5081-4542-4 (library binding)
 1. Robotics—Juvenile literature. 2. Robotics—Vocational guidance—Juvenile literature. 3. Robots—Juvenile literature. I. Title. II. Series: Engineers rule!
 TJ211.2.F38 2016
 629.8'92—dc23
                          2015031617

Manufactured in the United States of America

CPSIA Compliance Information: Batch #BW16PK: For Further Information contact Rosen Publishing, New York, New York at 1-800-237-9932

CONTENTS

SCIENCE FICTION VS. FACT

For a long time, robots were simply something that lived in the imagination of science fiction writers. The earliest robots looked nothing like the **androids** and **automatons** we see in movies, television shows, and comic books. However, the second half of the 1900s saw huge advancements in science and **technology**. These advancements led to the development of robots that were more **complex** than anything that came before them.

From the giant machines that build our cars to the small devices that clean our floors, robots come in all shapes and sizes. They're designed to help us in our everyday lives. Whatever a robot's size, shape, or function, it must first be designed, tested, and built. That's where robotic engineers come in.

Sometimes robots in movies move and behave just like people. While this is still science fiction, today's robotic engineers are working hard to design robots that are more humanlike.

BUMBLEBEE, *TRANSFORMERS*

ROBOCOP, *ROBOCOP*

C-3PO, *STAR WARS*

T-800, *TERMINATOR 2*

WHAT IS ROBOTIC ENGINEERING?

Robotic engineering is a career that deals with designing, constructing, and operating robots. Robotic engineers also design and develop the computer systems needed to control and operate robots properly. Because designing and building robots is a complex job, robotic engineering combines skills from many different fields, such as **mechanical** engineering, electrical engineering, and computer science. Some engineers even draw inspiration from biologists to design robots that act like living organisms.

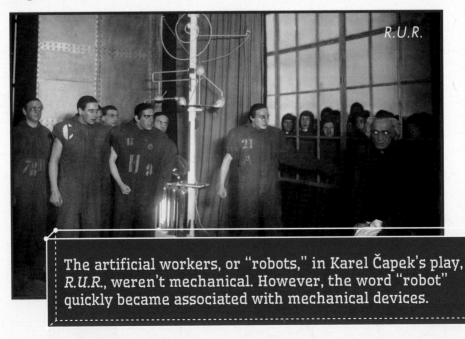

R.U.R.

The artificial workers, or "robots," in Karel Čapek's play, *R.U.R.*, weren't mechanical. However, the word "robot" quickly became associated with mechanical devices.

ROSSUM'S UNIVERSAL ROBOTS

The word "robot" first appeared in 1921. That year, Czech writer Karol Čapek published the play *R.U.R. (Rossum's Universal Robots)*. The play opens in a factory that makes artificial creatures called "robots" that look just like people. The word was based on the Slavic word *rabota*, which means "forced labor." Before Čapek's play, self-operating machines were called "automata" or "automatons."

Robotics is a rapidly growing field. As technology advances, engineers are able to research, design, and build new kinds of robots to serve a wide variety of purposes in homes, factories, and on the battlefield. If a job is too dangerous, boring, or dirty for a human, there's probably a robot that can do it.

HISTORY OF ROBOTS

Believe it or not, the idea of artificial, or man-made, beings has been around for thousands of years. Many ancient societies have myths and legends about self-moving machines and devices. The Greek god Hephaestus was said to have created three-legged tables that could move around on their own. A story from India tells of a king's underground treasure that's guarded by robots.

In the 4th century BC, a Greek mathematician named Archytas designed a mechanical, steam-propelled bird called "The Pigeon." In the 1100s, a Muslim inventor named al-Jazari built a number of automated machines, including water-powered robots that could play musical instruments. In 1495, Leonardo da Vinci designed a mechanical knight that could sit up, wave its arms, and move its head.

Leonardo da Vinci's mechanical knight was designed based on his artistic studies of the human body. In 2002, robotic engineer Mark Rosheim built a model using da Vinci's original designs.

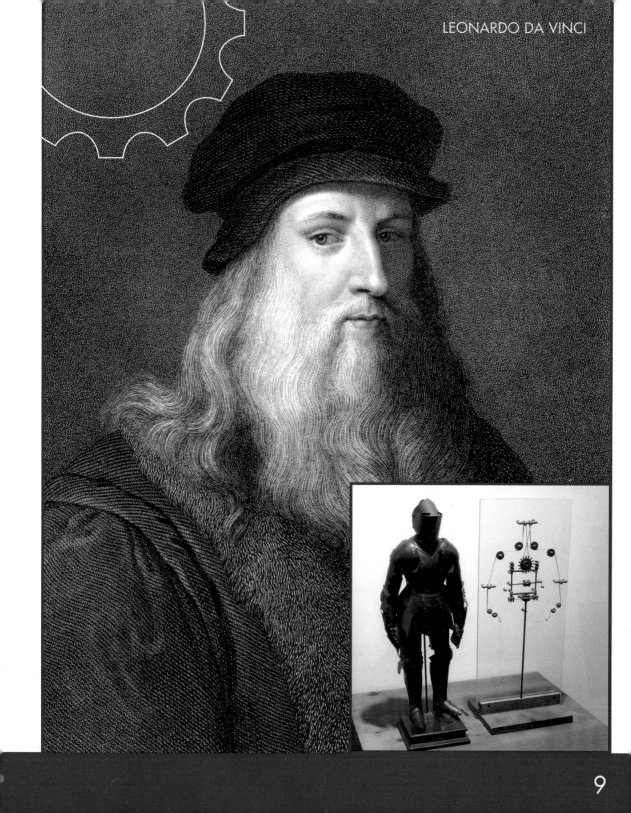

As time went on, people continued to design and construct mechanical devices that could move, fly, and play music. In 1737, Jacques de Vaucanson built "The Digesting Duck," a mechanical duck that could flap its wings and eat grain. The **Industrial Revolution** brought numerous technological advances that would lead to the development of today's modern robots.

Two early advances that benefited the field of robotic engineering were electricity and radio. Historical robots were powered by water, steam, or clockwork. Electrical motors and batteries allowed for more complex machines. In 1898, scientist and inventor Nikola Tesla developed a way to use radio waves to operate a device remotely. Wireless control would allow robots to operate at greater distances from those who controlled them.

NEW YORK WORLD'S FAIR

TIMELINE OF ROBOTICS

c. 420 BC
Archytas invents "The Pigeon,"
a wooden, steam-propelled bird.

1495
Leonardo da Vinci designs
a humanlike robot.

1737
Jacques de Vaucanson builds
a mechanical duck.

1921
Karel Čapek writes *R.U.R.*
(Rossum's Universal Robots),
marking the first time the word
"robot" is used.

1939
Westinghouse Electric Corporation
exhibits a humanlike robot at the
New York World's Fair.

1961
The first industrial robot is used
in a General Motors factory.

1977
Victor Scheinman sells his design for
the first programmable robot arm to
Unimation. Unimation develops the
robot arm, calling it PUMA.

1999
AIBO, a robotic dog capable of
interacting with its owner,
is released.

2002
The Roomba robotic vacuum
cleaner is introduced.

2014
ReWalk is approved for use
in home and public. ReWalk
uses powered leg attachments to
help people walk when they're
unable to.

Before the 1900s, most mechanical automatons
were little more than expensive toys used by
wealthy people to amuse and amaze guests.

Robotics combines skills and knowledge from many different **disciplines**. Because of this, robotic engineers can work in many different fields. One branch of robotic engineering works on locomotion, or how a robot moves. Many robots move using wheels, but this makes moving across uneven, rocky ground or going

up or down stairs impossible. Engineers who study robot locomotion try to design mechanisms that help robots move more efficiently, especially on uneven land. Some engineers study living things, such as insects, to develop new ways for robots to move.

Microrobotics and nanorobotics both deal with small-scale robots. Microrobotic engineers may design miniature robots used in surgery or insect-sized **drones** used by the military.

Nanorobotics deals with creating robots that are the size of molecules. Imagine a future where nanorobots can be used to fight diseases from inside our bodies. Thanks to robotic engineers, that day may become a reality.

THE THREE LAWS OF ROBOTICS

In 1942, author Isaac Asimov published a short story titled "Runaround." In this story, Asimov created the Three Laws of Robotics.

1. A robot may not injure a human being or, through inaction, allow a human being to come to harm.
2. A robot must obey any orders given to it by human beings, except where such orders would conflict with the First Law.
3. A robot must protect its own existence as long as such protection does not conflict with the First or Second Law.

Do you think it's possible for a machine to think? Artificial intelligence, or AI, is the branch of computer science that attempts to create intelligent machines. Robotic engineers who work in artificial intelligence are trying to design machines that can think like living things, as well as interact with their environment, or surroundings. Scientists hope that research in artificial intelligence will lead to robots that can think, plan, learn, and communicate.

Android science is one of the newest branches of robotic engineering. Android science studies human and robot interaction based on the idea that a very humanlike robot, or android, can engage in more human social interactions with people. Movies such as *AI* and *Bicentennial Man* have attempted to guess what a world with thinking, feeling androids might be like.

BICENTENNIAL MAN

Robots in movies and television shows often look and act just like humans. Today's real robots aren't that advanced, but robotic engineers are hoping to change that.

THE TURING TEST

The Turing test was a test designed to determine a computer's ability to think and show intelligent behavior. A human judge is given a text-only conversation between a computer and a human. If the judge can't correctly tell which is the computer, then the computer is said to have passed the test. The test was created by Alan Turing, a British computer scientist who's considered the father of modern computing. At a competition in 2014, it was claimed a computer passed the test for the first time.

PARTS OF A ROBOT

Whatever a robot might look like, most share the same basic **components**. The basic parts of a robot are the sensors, effectors, actuators, and control systems.

Sensors are the parts of the robot that gather information about the robot's surroundings and help guide its behavior. Simple sensors, such as cameras and microphones, act as a robot's eyes and ears. Some robots have sensors that allow them to detect temperature and air pressure.

Effectors allow a robot to perform specific tasks. Claws, hammers, shovels, speakers, and screwdrivers are examples of effectors. Actuators are the motors that make the various parts of the robot move. The final component is the control system, which acts as the robot's brain.

Although robots are made of the same basic parts, it's how those parts work together that makes each robot different. A robot may have multiple sensors, effectors, and actuators to perform a specific task. Effectors may be different depending on the tasks the robot must perform.

INDUSTRIAL ROBOTS

The first widespread use of robots in the modern age was in manufacturing. Industrial robots are able to do jobs that are too boring or dangerous for human workers. They can also do the work more quickly and cheaply, with a single robot doing the job of multiple human workers.

Industrial robots tend to be rather simple. They're built to perform one or two jobs over and over again. Most industrial robots are little more than **articulated** arms designed to perform jobs like **welding**, painting, and assembling. Some industrial robots are used for product inspection and testing, while others are used for packaging, stacking, and loading products. Common effectors used on industrial robots include welding tools, spray guns, and gripping claws.

When most people think of industrial robots, they think of the robots used in factories, like this automobile factory. Each robot on the assembly line has one job, whether it's welding, painting, or screwing in nuts and bolts.

HOUSEHOLD ROBOTS

You've probably seen a science fiction movie where the future is full of robot servants. Although humanlike robot maids and butlers are still a thing of fiction, there are some robots available to do household chores.

Most household robots currently available are relatively simple in design. Some are capable of connecting to the Internet and can work on their own to a certain degree. Common household robots include robotic vacuum cleaners and floor cleaners. These robots use sensors to find dirty spots and avoid obstacles, such as furniture and stairs.

There are self-cleaning robotic litter boxes and security robots that can send alerts to their owners via email or text message. Outside the home, you can find robotic lawn mowers and pool cleaners. There are even robots that clean windows.

iRobot's Roomba robotic vacuum cleaners were first introduced in 2002. By 2013, 10 million units had been sold worldwide. The company even offers models that can be easily **customized** with cameras, lasers, and other devices.

ENTERTAINMENT ROBOTS

From the mechanical birds of the past to the robot pets of today, robots continue to serve as a source of pleasure. Theme parks around the world use complex, expensive robotics to create detailed, interactive rides and attractions. Robots are also used by the entertainment industry as both tools, such as computer-assisted cameras, and as props, such as the various androids seen in the popular *Star Wars* movies. Robots are also used as marketing tools, appearing at trade shows and conventions to show off a company's latest products.

Robot pets, especially dogs, have been popular toys for several decades. These robot pets are relatively cheap and can be programmed to perform various tricks. Newer, more expensive models are capable of interacting with the toy's owner.

Robot animals are nothing new. Many of the earliest mechanical figures were made to look like birds, horses, and other animals. Although a robot pet may never replace your dog or cat, they're still popular toys.

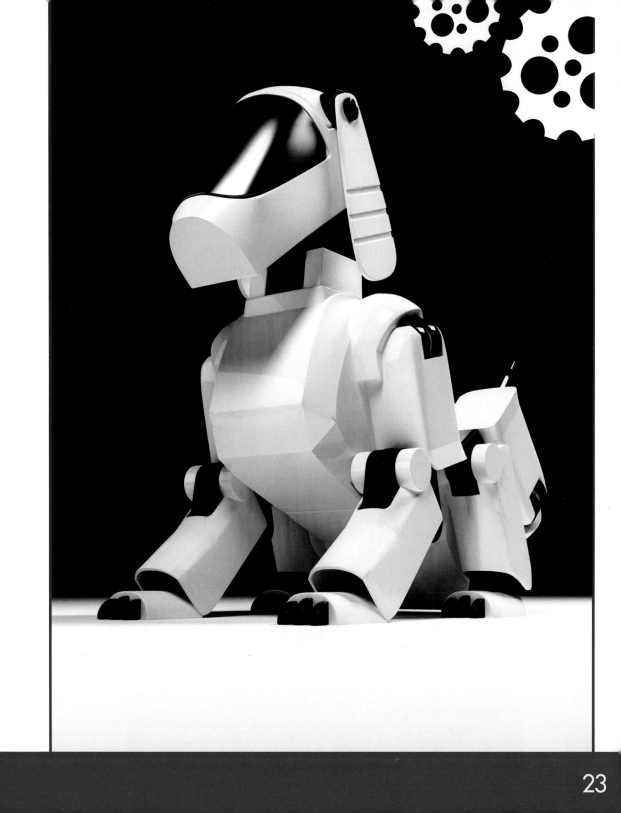

MEDICAL AND SCIENCE ROBOTS

Surgeons use medical robots to better reach the body parts they're operating on. Medical robots also help doctors operate on a patient from a distance, which is known as remote surgery. Surgical robots allow surgeons to be more precise and less **invasive**. Some hospitals also use robots to help patients during recovery and physical therapy. Disinfection robots use a special kind of light—ultraviolet—to fight dangerous viruses like Ebola.

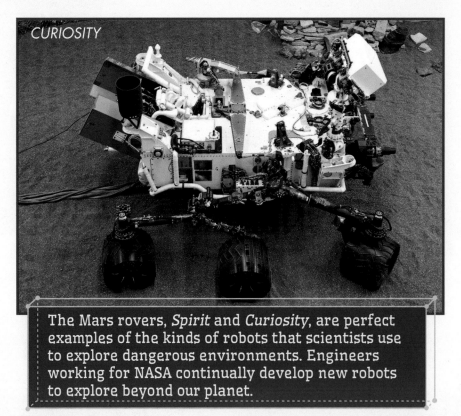

CURIOSITY

The Mars rovers, *Spirit* and *Curiosity*, are perfect examples of the kinds of robots that scientists use to explore dangerous environments. Engineers working for NASA continually develop new robots to explore beyond our planet.

There are even drone aircraft that have been used to deliver medicine and first aid supplies to people in out-of-the-way places.

Scientists use robots in various fields. Scientific robots are used to explore and investigate dangerous environments, such as volcanoes or the deep ocean. Scientists even use drones to study dangerous weather events, such as tornadoes and hurricanes.

ROBOTS IN THE MILITARY

Militaries have been using remote-controlled devices since World War II. Early examples of military robots were the remote-controlled tanks used by the German and Russian armies.

You might be familiar with military UAVs (unmanned aerial vehicles), such as the Reaper and Predator. However, the U.S. military uses other kinds of robots, too. Soldiers use robots with tank treads to explore dangerous areas, gather information, disarm or get rid of explosives, and even fight.

Engineers are constantly trying to think of new ways to use robots in order to save the lives of human soldiers. However, the Hollywood idea of robot armies meeting on the battlefield may never happen. There are strict rules in place about having humans make important military decisions—not robots.

One of a robot's main functions is to take the place of humans in dangerous situations. That's especially true of military robots.

PREDATOR

BECOMING A ROBOTIC ENGINEER

Robotic engineering is a difficult and rewarding career that takes a lot of studying and hard work. People who work in robotics need strong STEM skills. "STEM" stands for "science, technology, engineering, and math." If you're interested in pursuing a career in robotic engineering, you should take as many advanced STEM courses as you can in high school.

Entry-level robotic engineering jobs require a bachelor of science degree in robotics engineering, computer engineering, electrical engineering, or mechanical engineering. A robotic engineer can specialize in several different branches of engineering. Whichever branch you choose, robotic engineers typically take classes in advanced math, physical and life sciences, computer science, physics, and drafting. Since robotic engineers often work in groups, teamwork skills are important, too.

Robotic engineering is a fun and exciting career for people who love math and science. Working together, robotic engineers are designing our future.

Does robotic engineering sound like the right career for you? It can be a fun and rewarding career, but it takes a lot of study and hard work. There are things you can do right now to prepare for the future.

The first thing you could do is buy a robot kit at the nearest toy store or hobby shop. There are kits available for every level, from beginners to experts. You could join an after-school or community robotics club, or start one if a club doesn't already

exist. Many states offer specialized STEM or robotics summer camps, and some even have programs that run all year long. These programs are a great way to learn the basics of robotics and start your exciting engineering career.

GLOSSARY

android: A robot that looks like a person.

articulated: Having sections joined by joints.

automaton: Self-operating machines or mechanisms.

complex: Having many parts and thus not easy to understand or explain.

component: One of the parts of something.

customize: To make something to fit a user's needs or requirements.

discipline: A branch of knowledge or teaching.

drone: A pilotless aircraft.

Industrial Revolution: An era of social and economic change in the late 18th and 19th centuries marked by advances in technology and science.

invasive: Involving entry into the living body.

mechanical: Having to do with machines.

technology: The way people do something using tools and the tools that they use.

welding: A job that involves joining metal parts together by melting them.

INDEX

WEBSITES

Due to the changing nature of Internet links, PowerKids Press has developed an online list of websites related to the subject of this book. This site is updated regularly. Please use this link to access the list: www.powerkidslinks.com/engin/robot